I0478777

GET OUT OF DEBT

5 Crucial Lessons To Eliminate Debt, Start Accumulating Cash And Building A Solid Financial Future For You And Your Family

By Adam Watkins

CONTENTS

INTRODUCTION

I wanna thank you for purchasing this book. It is my mission to help you get out of debt and start enjoying financial security in life.

During the years, I've met so many people who told me they wanted to buy a new house or refinance their home. Unfortunately, many people were unable to qualify for a loan to purchase their own home due to their credit.

Looking at my clients' financial situations, I realized that most people lacked even the most essential financial knowledge. Things that I thought were so basic and necessary to qualify for a good loan, like having a good credit score, paying bills on time or not carrying a lot of credit card debt relative to your income to most people were revelations.

I will never forget a couple that came into my office looking to refinance their house.

Tom and Kimberley needed to lower their mortgage payment. Although they had two jobs each, they had a hard time coming up with the monthly payment. Tom even told me that he was considering looking for a third job that he could do for a few hours a week but he couldn't find one that would fit his already tight schedule. They had 4 kids and a ton of credit card debt.

Due to their low FICO (credit) score I could not find them a program that would fit their financial situation. After looking at their finances, I knew I had to help them somehow. It broke my heart to see the way they were living. They didn't see their kids much, relying on relatives to take care of them while they were working, sometimes for over 12 hours a day. I found myself teaching them how to pay off their debt. I showed them which credit cards they should be paying off first, I explained to them what compound interest is and how it was being used against them, and wrote down a detailed debt repayment plan.

When they left my office, they were hopeful and relieved, since now they had a plan to get out of their financial challenge. I did not create this plan I'm teaching today; I learned it, mastered it and taught countless people how to apply it successfully in order to change their financial situation.

Another case I have faced with is when a couple wanted to buy a $400,000 house. They had a combined income of $56,000 a year. They were both driving brand new cars, (they had paid $60,000 for those cars only a few months earlier) and their monthly car payments were just under $1200. On top of that, they also had $29,000 in credit card debt. Their mortgage monthly payment would have been $3,450. Incredibly, they couldn't understand why they were not approved for a loan.

A lady who came to me for advice admitted that the previous month she had been so upset with her husband for buying himself a new truck that she went to the dealership and bought herself a brand new car. Now they are having trouble paying for both cars.

These, along with other similar situations made me realize that most people were not taking credit card debts seriously. And the main reason was that they did not know exactly how the credit works. But that's only one part of the equation. The other part is that we live in such a consumerist society that no matter what you do or where you go, you are constantly exposed to advertisements. Whether you are watching TV, browsing the web, reading the paper or just driving around town, you are being bombarded with ads. And most importantly, many of those ads are targeting kids, so they grow up constantly thinking about spending money. And how many ads do you see which are about saving money? None.

The reason we don't know how the credit works is because nobody has ever explained it to us. Banks, credit card companies and mortgage companies would prefer that you never find out because it is in their best interest to keep you in debt. They only make money when you are in debt.

Once you read Part 1, you will never look at credit the same way again. Once you understand exactly how compound interest is being used against you, you will be shocked.

We need to take action now. We cannot rely on anybody to take care of us; we need to take care of ourselves. We cannot blame anybody for our situation. We need to take responsibility for what we have, what we don't have and where we are in life.

There are many books and resources out there that can teach you how to get out of debt, but this book is different, and that difference is a crucial one. Half of this book (parts 1 and 2) explains what credit is and how to get out of debt; the second half (parts 3 and 4) will show you how to change your mindset about money and how to change your limiting beliefs.

In my quest to understand why most people fail and only few succeed, I've realized that making money is easy, the problem is all the emotional garbage that we have around money. I am a firm believer that if people don't change their mindset about money, if they don't solve their issues about money, they will always have financial problems. Even if they win the lottery, if they don't know how to deal with money, sooner or later they will lose it all. We have seen this happen in countless examples of overnight millionaires which lost everything afterwards.

So my goal here is to provide you with a simple, step-by-step plan that will help you get out of debt, and also to provide you with the tools and motivation to change your mindset and your beliefs about money. This is, in my opinion, the best way to get out of debt ,stay out of debt forever, and start accumulating the wealth that you and your family deserve.

THE FIRST STEPS OF DEBT ELIMINATION

Depending upon your specific circumstances, there are distinctive ways to deal with escaping obligation. How about we examine them right now so you can choose which approach will work better for you, in view of where you are monetarily at this moment.

If you have been paying your bills on time and have a good credit record (and want to keep it in a good position), and you are working and have a monthly income, then you can follow the plan outlined in Part 2. Credit Counseling or Debt Settlement will not be a good choice for you.

If your accounts are past due and you cannot make the payments, then the Credit Counseling (also commonly known as Debt Management or Debt Consolidation) or the Debt Settlement might be a good choice for you. You can go to Part 3 for more information on these services.

It's important to note that there is no magic bullet that will work for every debt situation. In any case, remember that much of the time, cash issues are NOT the consequence of budgetary issues but instead an aftereffect of how we think.

This may sound esoteric to some people, but when you think about it you will realize that it is true. For example, take any self-made millionaire, somebody that went from poverty to millionaire by himself or herself. If you were to take all their money away, do you think they can make it back? You bet! The reason is that they have a different set of beliefs about what is possible in life, they think differently than most people.

And when you consider that most people that won the lottery lost it all within just a couple of years, then you can see that how we think and what we believe is possible for us makes all the difference in the world.

I don't believe in luck. I don't believe that we are like a leaf in the wind that goes where the wind blows, with no control whatsoever over what is possible. I used to think that way, but not anymore. I believe that we are all in charge of our lives and in charge of our destinies. And I invite you to try this approach in your life, and discover that in reality, you truly are in charge of your destiny. Anything is possible for you, no matter how the economy is doing or what is going on around you.

This is the main reason I included the section about how to change your limiting beliefs in this book. Even if you manage to get out of debt without changing your beliefs about what is possible for you, then there is a very high chance that you may get back in debt in the near future. And I sincerely want you to live a successful, happy life that I strongly believe is your birthright.

There is so much abundance around us all the time, yet we fail to appreciate it. Instead, we are taught from an early age that all supplies are limited. Limited jobs, limited opportunities, limited money, limited everything! Then no wonder when we analyze our belief systems -see Part 4- all kinds of limiting beliefs start popping up that we never knew we had, but we have been blindly guiding everything we did in our lives since we were little kids.

I sincerely want you to become debt-free as soon as possible, because I believe that being in debt is being in financial slavery. It limits everything you do in your life going from whether you will send your kids to private or public school and the education they will receive, the area of town and the house you will live in all the way even to the medical insurance you will get! When you are in a good financial situation, you have many more choices available to you. Living in poverty is NOT the solution to the world's problems.

Now it's time to begin your journey. If you are ready to become debt free and live a financially stress-free life, turn the page over to Part One, where I discuss what credit is and how it can either destroy you or make you rich, depending on how you use it. You will learn what banks and financial institutions don't want you to know…

LESSON #1

UNDERSTANDING HOW & WHY CREDIT REALLY SLOWS YOU DOWN

"Money is in some respects like fire; it is a very excellent servant but a terrible master. When you have it mastering you; when interest is constantly piling up against you, it will keep you down in the worst kind of slavery. But let money work for you, and you have the most devoted servant in the world. It is no "eye-servant." There is nothing animate or inanimate that will work so faithfully as money when placed at interest, well secured. It works night and day, and in wet or dry weather."

– P.T Barnum, The Art of Money Getting.

HOW CREDIT CARDS REALLY WORK

If you want to eliminate your credit card debt you have to understand what credit is.

In case you haven't figured it out yet, the credit system works against you, unless you are prepared.

And since it is an unfair game, you need to know the rules. Once you understand how credit works, how compound interest works, you can start using it to your advantage, instead of being a victim of it.

Here are some facts you need to know.

In 2005, a record 6 billion "pre-approved" credit card offers were mailed to consumers. By comparison, only 10 years before, in 1995, 2.7 billion offers were mailed out.

These offers usually carry a "low introductory" rate which is "fixed" for a set number of months. But, once you read the fine print, you find out that in reality that "fixed" rate can change at any time, and for any reason.

Let's look at an example: "Rates, Fees and terms may change: We reserve the right to change the terms of your account (including the APRs) at any time, for any reason, in addition to APR increases that may occur for failure to comply with the terms of your account" (underlying is mine)

So you may be thinking you are getting a great deal, when in reality they can change the rules whenever they want.

Unfortunately, you cannot beat the system. They write the rules to their advantage and we must comply. Every year, credit card companies, banks and financial institutions spend millions and millions of dollars lobbying Congress to make sure the laws that are passed benefit them and not the consumers.

YOU SIMPLY CANNOT COMPETE

The good news is that you don't need to beat the system; you just need to understand it.

Pre-approved offers are mailed to anyone on a list that a credit card company purchases (usually from the Credit Bureaus), and does not mean that you will definitely get a credit card. They are inviting you to apply, but they are targeting their mailings towards consumers who are more likely to respond and qualify for a card.

If you do not want to receive any more offers, you can call (888)567-8688 to request that Credit Bureaus not include your file in any pre-approved / promotional lists. I encourage you to opt-out, if (for no other reason) you want to minimize the chances of identity theft.

If you prefer to contact the Bureaus directly, write to the following addresses and tell them you want to opt-out of pre-approval screening:

```
Equifax Options:
P O Box 7401243 - Atlanta, GA 30374-0123 (800)556-4711
Experian Consumer Opt Out
701 Experian Parkway - Allen, TX 75013 (800)353-0809
TransUnion
Attn: Marketing Opt Out – PO Box 97328 – Jackson, MS 39288-
7328
(800) 680-7293
```

There are several more practices that have become more common in the last few years.

One of them is the "Grace Period", which is the number of days you have to repay your purchase before you are charged interest. Many cards have reduced the grace period from 30 days down to 21 days. With a 21-day grace period you have less time to pay for your purchases in full, and a better chance of paying interest than before. And, if the amount is not paid in full, interest is charged from the date of purchase, not the day you started financing it.

Another practice is the addition of the over-the-limit fee. Many consumers would expect their credit card to be declined if a transaction would put the card over their credit limit. But, increasingly, credit card companies are allowing these transactions to go through, then slapping consumers with an over-the-limit fee of $20, $25 or more.

Late fees are escalating too, adding $30 to $50 to your credit card bill. Not to mention that your interest rate skyrockets. I personally know someone in New York who sent his payment in late, and his interest rate went from 9% to 29% the following month. This is very common.

There is likewise the Foreign Transaction expense that you get hit with while pulling back your cash from an ATM outside of the States. Keep that in mind next time you travel.

Simply withdrawing money from an ATM that doesn't belong to the bank means you are going to be hit with two fees. One fee that is charged by the bank that owns the ATM, and another fee that is charged by your bank (not all banks will charge this fee, but most will). Withdrawing $20 from another bank's ATM could result in $4 to $6 in fees. How many times a year do you withdraw money from other bank's ATMs?

There are way too many fees to list here, but you get the idea.

Are you asking yourself what you can do to protect yourself?

There are a number of things you can do.

First, you need to check your credit card statements every month. Believe it or not, most people do not check their statements. Check not only your credit card statements but also your checking account and your savings account statements. Search for any mistakes.

Look for fees, and see if they are correct. If you see any over-the-limit or late fees, call the company and ask (politely) if they can waive them. They will usually waive them, but if you are late again or over the limit again, they may not do it a second time.

Be very careful when mailing your payments. Send them at least 10 days before the due date to avoid late fees. Or set it up so the balance is deducted from your checking or savings account automatically. Contact your bank to find out how to do it.

You can also (and I encourage you to do this) call your credit card companies and ask for a reduction of your interest rate. This may be a little harder to get, but if they don't want to do it, don't despair. Call again in a couple of weeks, and ask again. In Part 2 you can read a script you can use when you call.

WHAT IS SO IMPORTANT ABOUT COMPOUND INTEREST?

""Compound interest is the eighth wonder of the world. He who understands it, earns it ... he who doesn't ... pays it." - Albert Einstein

This is the most important concept to understand if you plan to stay debt free forever.

And for you to understand exactly how it works, I'll ask you a question: What would you rather have, a million dollars in cash right now, or one penny today, two pennies tomorrow, four pennies the next day, eight pennies the next one and so on for the next 30 days?

Most people would choose the million dollars, and it is a good choice, I mean, who wouldn't want a million dollars? However, the second option is much better. Look at the following table to see the power of compound interest in action:

Day	1	$.01
Day	2	$.02
Day	3	$.04
Day	4	$.08
Day	5	$.16
Day	6	$.32
Day	7	$.64
Day	8	$1.28
Day	9	$2.56
Day	10	$5.12
Day	11	$10.24
Day	12	$20.48
Day	13	$40.96
Day	14	$81.92
Day	15	$163.84
Day	16	$327.68
Day	17	$655.36
Day	18	$1,310.72
Day	19	$2,621.44
Day	20	$5,242.88

Day	21	$10,485.76
Day	22	$20,971.52
Day	23	$41,943.04
Day	24	$83,386.08
Day	25	$167,772.16
Day	26	$335,544.32
Day	27	$671,088.64
Day	28	$1,342,177.28
Day	29	$2,684,354.56
Day	31	$5,368,709.12

This is the magic of compound interest. A penny doubled every day may not seem like much, but the compounding factor is incredible. In fact, Albert Einstein has also been quoted as saying *"The most powerful force in the universe is compound interest."*

As you can see in the table above, a penny doubled every day gives you over $5,000,000 in just 30 days. This is how powerful compound interest is. And this is what credit card companies are using against you.

When you make charges on your credit card, you pay interest on any adjust you convey (balance would be any unpaid amount on your credit card statement). This interest is calculated not only on the initial principal but also the accumulated interest of prior periods.

Compound interest can really hurt you, especially if you are making the minimum payment on each of your credit cards. When you carry a balance, compound interest is calculated daily, which means every day interest is added to your balance. If you pay the minimum payment on a credit card, you are only making the bank richer.

To show you compound interest in action, consider that if you have a credit card with $5,000 balance at 18% a year, and you were to pay only the minimum payment (let's say it's 3% of your balance), it would take you 199 months to pay it off! (Assuming that the rate doesn't change and you never use your card again). So your account will be paid off in exactly 199 months (over 16 years!) and you will have paid $4,698.46 in interest. This is insane. This is what banks don't want you to know. Send them only the minimum payment and they will love you forever.

(Source:http://www.bankrate.com/calculators/managing-debt/minimum-payment-calculator.aspx)

HOW HOME MORTGAGE LOANS REALLY WORK

If you have your own home you may not even think of your mortgage as debt. You may even believe that the house is truly yours. You need to understand how mortgage loans work if you want to really be debt-free.

Home mortgages operate the same way that credit cards do. The difference is that mortgage companies will never say that the interest on their loans is compounded daily (maybe on their fine print, buried among hundreds of pages that you sign at closing). In any case, now that you see how compound interest functions, you may begin to understand that it just bodes well to pay off your home loan at the earliest opportunity.

Most people just assume that the interest on their mortgage is simple interest. When they get a 6% interest rate, they think that the interest they pay will be 6% of the total amount they financed, calculated yearly. This is what I found out after talking to my clients. Nothing could be further from the actual truth. In reality, if you paid off your whole mortgage in one year, then yes, the interest rate would be 6% (well, actually a little more because of the compounding effect, but I'm trying to illustrate a point here). But if it is paid over 30 years, then the actual interest rate is well over 100%! Think about it! You could buy more than 2 houses with the same money!

Loan Amount	Interest Rate	Term	Monthly Payment	Total Paid (Principal + Interest)	Interest Paid
$200,000	6%	30 years, fixed	$1199.10	$431,676.80	$231,676.38

The reason that the interest rate is so important is that you're paying compound interest, not simple interest. The higher the interest rate, then obviously, the more interest you will pay. I have seen people with a 9.8% interest on their $300,000 loan; in 30 years they will have paid over $631,000 in interest alone! That's over 200% interest!

These examples are worrisome; however, they do not compare to the other types of mortgage loans that are causing so many people lose their homes.

One of them is the so called "Interest Only" loans. Basically you only pay the interest portion of the payment, deferring the difference (thereby accumulating interest, which is added to your account). It means that you aren't only NOT paying down the balance of your loan, but you are also adding more interest (you are adding interest to the balance you didn't yet pay). If property values are going up, then it may not be a bad loan in some specific cases (i.e., buying a house with the intention of selling it in a few months); however, in a declining market it is financial suicide. The only way somebody would benefit from an Interest Only mortgage loan is if they were sending some money to be applied towards the principal every month and the interest rate would be substantially lower than they had before (if they are refinancing). On purchases it was a good option when houses were appreciating very fast, as was the case in many parts of the country not too long ago, but obviously very risky. In today's market, it's definitely not an option to consider.

The riskiest mortgage loans available are called <u>Option ARM</u> (Adjustable Rate Mortgage) or Pick A Pay loans. Consistently, you get the chance to pick whichpayment (out of four) you will send to the home loan organization. This is a good option for professionals or business owners whose income fluctuates sharply from month to month, but <u>definitely NOT</u> for most people.

With **option 1** you send <u>less</u> than that month's interest (which means, <u>the difference is added to the balance, collecting more interest.</u>) For example, let's take a $200,000 loan with a Fully Amortizing rate (the real rate that would pay off the loan in 30 years) of 7.683% and a minimum payment rate of 1.25%. **The option one payment will be $666.50** (deferring $614 of the interest that was due that month, which automatically is added to the balance and starts collecting interest)

With **option 2**, you send <u>only the interest for that month</u> (which means, you are <u>not</u> paying down the balance, or explained differently, it's as if you were like "renting" the house!

Following the previous example, you would send **$1,280.60** for that month, but the balance would not be paid down.

With **option 3**, you send the regular payment (principal and interest) calculated over 30 years. In this example, it would be **$1,423.58.**

And with **option 4** you send the regular payment calculated over 15 years instead of 30, but it will be obviously substantially higher. Following our example that payment would be **$1,874.88**

CAN YOU GUESS WHICH PAYMENT MOST PEOPLE USUALLY SEND?

I have seen mortgage statements from banks where the option that is highlighted in the payment coupon (or in big, bold letters) is always the minimum payment (option 1). This leads a massive amount of people to believe that's the payment they should send, and many people usually send just that. One of my clients added $60,000 to his mortgage loan in just 2 ½ years without having any idea what's actually going on. In my experience, many people were not well informed when they were offered these loans.

Option Arm loans can spell trouble, especially when property values decline and home owners owe more than their house is worth. To add insult to injury, when people refinance they discover that the interest rate is always higher on an Option Arm loan than on a 30-year fixed loan! Fortunately, these types of loans are not so popular in the US right now as they were in the early 2000's.

IGNORANCE IS NOT BLISS, IT IS HIGHLY EXPENSIVE

Many people believe that paying off their mortgage is a bad financial decision, and they have two arguments to back up this position. I respect both arguments, but I do not agree with either one. The first argument is that a home mortgage has a lot of financial benefits (since mortgage interest can be deducted from your taxes); the second is that since the interest on a mortgage is usually low (around 4 to 6% in the last few years depending on many factors like your credit, etc), you will benefit by making regular payments to your mortgage lender and investing your discretionary income elsewhere, as long as the interest on your investment is higher than the interest on your mortgage.

Let's take a look at both arguments. As far as the mortgage interest being tax deductible, what it really means is that if you pay, let's say, $10,000 in mortgage interest in a given year, you will save up to $2,500 in taxes (if you are at a 25% bracket; it would be even less money if you are at a lower bracket!). Think about this for a moment. Does it really make financial sense to you? Paying the bank $10,000 to get back $2,500? If you are like me, it will not make any sense at all. It makes more sense to pay off the mortgage, and once it's paid off, you get to KEEP the $10,000 (or whatever you would have paid in interest) as a disposable income or as investment money.

As far as investing your money somewhere else that could give you a higher return (higher than your mortgage interest), let me offer you the following facts: whatever interest you pay on your mortgage, it will be the <u>GUARANTEED</u> interest you will make by paying it off (or paying it down). You cannot guarantee the performance of any other investment, as you probably already know. Market conditions fluctuate and could affect your investments; however, paying off your 6% mortgage is a guaranteed 6 % "return".

And let's face it, most people, including myself, are not keen investors. Many will have a Mutual Fund or retirement account that they rarely review, and investing does take a lot of planning and research. Without proper planning and research you could be "throwing darts" at your financial future. When you consider this, then paying off your mortgage early does make financial sense due to its simplicity and high return. Be that as it may, on the off chance that you are a sharp financial specialist, then it might bode well not to pay off your home loan and contribute your discretionary salary elsewhere.

In the next part, I will show you a way to pay off ALL your debt, including your mortgage, in record time. This method is not about refinancing your home, it is not about debt consolidation, nor is it about debt settlement. It is based on a surprisingly simple (and incredibly powerful) formula that will give you the financial freedom you and your family deserve. This system will work even if you are under a debt consolidation program or if you have student loans.

LESSON #2

15 SIMPLE (YET EFFECTIVE) WAYS TO LOWERING YOUR EXPENSES

(AND SAVE SOME SERIOUS CASH IN THE PROCESS...)

We live in a society where we learned to spend all the money we make. We make $2000 a month, and we spend it all. We get a better paying job and start making $3000 a month, and guess what, we spend $3000 a month. The US Savings rate is at an all-time low, as more people are in debt than ever before.

Times are tough for most people in the US, and we know that our lives would be much better with an extra $200, $300 or more per month. I can't help you get a better job, but I can help you identify areas where you can start saving money starting today. In some areas you'll notice that your savings will be small and in others will be really significant. In any case, it's more money in your pocket that you can save or spend any which way you want!

So let's dive into it. You may want to read this report thoroughly to have an idea of the savings you can get, and then read it again and start implementing these ideas. It will certainly not help you to just read it and do nothing about it. Please put it into action and don't delay, start as soon as possible. The sooner you start, the more money you will have by the end of this month!

MY 15 STEPS PLAN TO BECOMING A LEAN, MEAN EXPENSE-CUTTING MACHINE...

1- Saving money on your monthly television expenses is an easy way to cut costs. Are you still paying for cable or satellite television? Switching to a lower priced plan with less channels can save you between $15 and $40, or you can disconnect it altogether and get hulu.com or Netflix for movies.

I've disconnected my cable TV service about two years ago, and I do not miss it a bit. What's more, my kids don't even ask for it, which was a concern I had when I was considering canceling the service. I used to pay $45 a month, now I am saving $45 x12: $540 a year.

2-Do you drink coffee at Starbucks? If you do, how much do you spend a week? Multiply that amount times 52, that's how much you spend a year on coffee. You may want to consider switching to Dunkin Donuts Coffee and save (on average) $131 a year, or make coffee at home or at the office and save even more!

I am not a Starbucks client, but I used to eat a bagel with cream cheese every week at Bagel Brothers. Not a whole lot, but at $2.65 per bagel (including tax) that I gave up, I am now saving $138 a year. Some may say it is not much, but everything adds up.

3- Are you still using regular light bulbs? You may want to switch to energy-efficient light bulbs that will last longer and save money on the electric bill (20 light bulbs can save up to $166 a year). I replaced all my lights for energy efficient bulbs, but I cannot measure my savings as it didn't occur to me to keep track.

4- Drop your regular cell phone plan and switch to a prepaid plan. These days, all big companies offer a prepaid option, with savings of up to $30 a month ($360 a year!) for the same or very similar service.   And the smaller companies (MetroPCS, Cricket, etc) all offer great savings compared to Verizon, ATT and Sprint.

Unless you are still under contract and you would pay a hefty early termination fee, it doesn't make any sense to get a new plan every two years just to get a new phone. You are wasting a lot of money that could be better used elsewhere (like paying off debt!).

I bought my phone through Craigslist and I'm still using an old plan for $40 a month (1000 minutes and 400 texts, with no data). Most people on average spend about $75 a month on cell phone, so I'm saving $35 a month, times 12: $420 a year. I would go with a pre-paid option if I need data, which I don't need right now. Here you can save some good money, especially if there are two or three phones in your household.

5- Do you need to buy medications? Choose generic medications and save a lot of money! Just because it's made from a well-known pharmaceutical company doesn't mean it's better than the one made by CVS or RightAid or your local drugstore. You'll be amazed at the price difference, so don't overlook this savings opportunity next time you need to by medications. I haven't bought the pharmaceutical version of the medicine I needed in years.

6- Do you go to the movies? It's expensive, isn't it? I mean, two people can easily spend $40 to $50 dollars in a couple of hours with the tickets, pop corn and soda! How about watching a movie at home? Just prepare some popcorn (or buy ice cream) and still have a good time, while saving a lot of money. It may not be the latest movie that just came out, but I'm sure you didn't watch all movies that came out in the last few years, so you can easily find a good one you haven't watched yet. I am not saying never go to the movies ever again, but every so often choose the "movie at home" option, and save the money. Heck, Redbox rents movies for $1.29, compare that to $24 for two movie tickets!

7- Do you have Internet cable or DSL at home? Call your internet service provider and ask for a cheaper option. When I called, they switched me to a slightly slower plan that saves me $7 a month, and I didn't notice the difference in speed. That's $84 a year!

8- Do you carry a balance on your credit cards? No matter what your balance is or what your interest rate is, call ALL your credit card companies and ask them to reduce the rate. Be very polite when you call, and if they decline to lower your rate, call again in a few days. Many times (and I do mean, many times) they will reduce the rate for you unless you are delinquent or have not been sending the payments on time. Even if you haven't been consistent with your payments, call anyway. You may be surprised. When I called, not only did they reduce my rate, but they also increased my credit limit (and I didn't even ask for it). The savings here can be substantial, depending on the rate you get and how much you owe. Do not overlook this option, as I have heard of many people getting their rates reduced with just a simple phone call. That translates into more money in your pocket!

9- Another easy way to lower your monthly payments: call other insurance companies (car and/or house insurance if you own your home) and compare their prices with what you are paying right now, and switch to the one that offers you the best option for the same coverage you currently have.

I saved over $500 a year by switching car insurance companies a few years ago, and then after two years, I switched again just to save another $175 a year. Please do this, it does take a little time to do the research, but you can save some good money.

10- Do you still have a landline telephone service at home? Then you have a few options for saving money. If you have a cell phone, then consider cancelling your home service (savings: $15 to $25 a month). Or, cancel add-ons like caller ID and other services and save $4-$6 a month. Or, switch to a company like Ooma (the one I use) for about $100 for the telephone device and get free monthly service with unlimited long distance (within the US) and many freebies like caller ID (just pay a couple of dollars in taxes). So all I pay for my home phone service is less than $3 a month for the taxes, with unlimited calling. You do need a high speed internet connection for Ooma to work for you. Another option is MagicJack, for about $20 a year for service. I sent a MagicJack device to my mother who lives overseas, and we talk almost every day for as long as we want. My savings? About $50 a month in International Long Distance calling, or $600 a year. Plus the money my mom saves because she doesn't pay to call me anymore.

By now you can clearly see how much all these savings add up. But keep reading for more savings!

11- Are you financing your car? If so, have you thought about refinancing it? Shop around for rates to see if you can lower your monthly payments without extending the life of your loan by getting a cheaper rate. You have to consider the costs involved to see if in your case it would make sense to go through the process.

Some people have saved some decent money by getting a loan from Credit Union that was substantially better than the one they got from the car dealer when they purchased their vehicle. Remember that the dealership gets a cut on the loan they offer you, which could be your savings by choosing to go with Credit Union.

12- Are you a homeowner? You can check out whether refinancing your home would make sense for you in your particular situation, as the mortgage rates are at historically low levels (low like 3.5 or 4% on a 30 year fixed loan, depending on credit rating and other factors). You have to calculate how you're your closing costs would be to see whether you will save money or not. But if you can get a rate that is two points (or more) lower than your current rate, you can save a lot of money over the life of your loan.

Be careful though: to compare apples to apples, calculate the new loan over the same amount of months you have left over on your current loan; I mean if you still have 25 years to pay off your current loan, make the new loan for 25 years and not for 30.

13- Do you buy books or subscribe to magazines? Then you can save money by borrowing books from the Public Library where you can also read Consumer Reports, People, Oprah and other popular magazines for free.

14- Do you bank with one of the bigger banks, like Chase, Bank of America and so on? You may want to look into smaller Credit Unions, as their fees are substantially lower and their rates are almost always better. Banks make most of their money by charging hefty fees (withdraw $20 from another bank's ATM and you will pay between $4 and $6 in fees - just to withdraw your OWN money! Remember that you pay a fee to the Bank that owns the ATM as well as to your own bank.)

Switching to a local Credit Union almost ALWAYS makes financial sense. Look at a bank statement and add up all charges by your bank in any given month. They are unbelievable! Once you switch, you'll be so glad you did.

15- If you own your home, you may want to invest about $35 in a programmable thermostat that will allow you to save a considerable amount of money in your monthly bill via a better control of the heating and cooling of your home. This is not easy to measure as far as how much you will save, but you will have enormous saves.

Bonus tip: This is one of the greatest cash channels for the vast majority. How regularly do you eat out or arrange sustenance at a fast food place or eatery? The money we (in America) spend eating out amounts to billions a year (my guess, with no scientific evidence ☺). But think about it: if you pay for food every day at work (instead of bagging your own food from home), you are wasting hundreds of dollars a month. Do some easy math: if you spend, let's say $5 a day eating out (I know, most people spend close to $10, after all, what can you eat for $5?) it amounts to $25 a week, times 52 is $1300 a year. If you bag your food instead, you will save at least half of it, and you will also eat healthier.

Or, if you eat out with your family on a regular basis, try to at least cut it down as much as possible. Food for four people at a restaurant will cost at least $50 (many times much more). If you avoid it at least 5 times a year by choosing to eat at home, you will save another $250 a year.

LESSON #3

HOW TO GET OUT OF DEBT:
THE STEP-BY-STEP PLAN

If you are ready to become debt-free, here is an effective, proven strategy that will help you get out of debt in an organized way. Following the step-by-step plan will get you out of debt in record time.

Step 1- You have to absolutely, totally, 100%, commit yourself to getting out of debt - and commit yourself to following your plan, no matter what happens.

This may seem obvious, but the only way you are going to succeed is if you are 100% committed to your debt elimination plan. Anthony Robbins, well known motivational speaker, says that it's in the moments of decisions that our destinies are shaped. Decide TODAY you are going to make it happen. Do not take this step lightly. You will not succeed unless you commit yourself. It may help to get a buddy to keep you on track.

If you ask a successful dieter how they lost the weight and kept if off, they will tell you that it was not by starving themselves, but by committing to a sensible plan. It is that commitment that gets you back on the horse if you fall off the wagon.

Step2- Stop charging your credit cards as of today!

Your main goal right now is to get out of debt as soon as possible. So you <u>must</u> cut your spending. I know this is tough to do, but you have to cut your credit cards. (Keep one in case of an emergency.) If you are truly committed, stop reading and start cutting. To get out of debt, you will need to change your habits. Your old habits will not work!

The sacrifices you make now will have an incredible benefit in the long term. From now on, if you cannot pay cash for something, don't buy it.

Step3- Find out where your money is going. You need to know <u>exactly</u> where your money is going and what your expenses are.

You can use a program like Quicken, AceMoney Lite (free), or similar software to track your money. Use a notepad, a pen and calculator if you don't have a computer.

You must write down ALL your expenses so you can determine exactly where your money is going. Convey with you a piece of paper where you can record all your money costs. They are usually the hardest to track but add up very quickly. Did you buy candy and a soda when you filled up your tank? Write it down.

Example of a Daily Record

Thursday, February 12

Coffee & pastry	$3.50
Lunch at "Abe's"	$7.90
"peeps" Magazine	$5.00
Soda Drink	$1.00
Vending machine snack	$1.00
Groceries	$76.85

The benefits of this log will be fantastic. Have you ever wondered what happened to that $20 bill you had in your pocket yesterday? It will never happen to you again, when you start to track your daily cash expenses.

At the end of the week, you will add all the numbers up so you can come up with your weekly expenses. This will be easy, once you have all your daily logs filled out.

Example of a Weekly Record

February 8-14

Breakfast	$17.50
Lunch	$42.00
Office Depot	$25.00
Entertainment	$14.00
Snacks	$12.00

Groceries	$126.85
Gasoline	$41.00

At the end of the month, add all your weekly records to come up with exactly how much money you spent that month.

Example of a Monthly Record

Spending Record - February

	week 1	week 2	week 3	week 4	TOTAL
Rent / Mortgage	1200				
Groceries	140	87	95	120	442
Lunch	42	46	53	30	171
Breakfast	17.5	22	16	18	34
Laundry	6	6	6	6	16
Gasoline	60	45	70	40	215
Gas & Electric	80	0	0	0	80
Entertainment	30	0	45	15	90
Cell Phone bill	0	0	80	0	80
Cable TV	76	0	0	0	76
Magazines	5	0	0	5	10
Newspaper	2	1.5	2	2	7.5
Office Depot	25	0	0	0	25
Fast Food	22	0	16	26	64
Pizza	12	12	0	0	24
Total					

Once you know where your money is going, look for places where you can "trim" your expenses. Some common examples are:

-Eating lunch out: at $8/day, it is around $200 per month. Some people spend $10 or $12 every day on lunch. Bag your lunch a few times a week.

-Going to Starbucks twice a week: if you only spend $6 a week, it would amount to $25 a month. Maybe you could skip it every now and then?

-Cable TV: Maybe you spend $80/month or more, when you could be paying $40 to $60 by eliminating channels you seldom watch.

-Occasional fast food: $25/week would mean $100/month.

-Magazine subscriptions you seldom read: Cancel them! Same with newspapers, music services, etc.

-Enjoy movies and popcorn at home instead of going out.

-Use coupons for groceries and buy store brands. Don't be tempted to buy something you don't need just because it's on sale. Also, beware of "bargains". If you are the type of person who is attracted to a "Sale" sign as if by a magnet, be aware that they are responsible for much impulse spending.

- Shop at consignment stores & discount stores like Ross or Marshalls (their clothes are usually good quality and people won't notice!)

- Cut down (or eliminate) sodas and snacks. They only make you fat, anyway.

- Eat frozen pizza at home instead of ordering out.

- Use your creativity! Where else could you save money? Remember, you do need to change your lifestyle if you want to make it happen.

- Call two or three car insurance companies and get new quotes. If you can lower your insurance payments through another company, then go ahead and switch! I saved over $600 a year with a 5 minute phone call.

Step 4- Develop a personal spending budget.

Consider this: most people spend more time planning a 3-day weekend than they do planning their life. By making a budget, you are committing yourself to getting out of debt, in writing. Use the budget spreadsheet you will find at the end of this book (under Resources) to prepare your budget.

Step5- Make a list of ALL your creditors (credit cards, department stores, etc) and call them.

You are going to ask them to lower your rate. This has worked amazingly well for many people, including myself. Here is a simple script you can use: "Hi, my name is [Your Name]. I am a good customer, but I have received several offers in the mail from other credit card companies with lower interest rates. I would like to see if you could lower the rate on my card, as it is a little high". If they say no, then say something like "I would hate to have to switch to another company after being with you for __ years… could you please check again, or could I please talk to your supervisor?" You can also ask to eliminate any fees they may have charged you recently (late fees, yearly fees, etc).

If your credit card company doesn't want to lower your rate, just try again a few days later. You can also say things like "What can you do to help me out?" or "Can you do any better?" For this strategy to work, you have to be polite, but firm. Never threaten, raise your voice or get angry.

Step 6- Open a savings account if you don't have one, and deposit money in it every month, before paying anyone else. This is a VITAL STEP. Don't brush it off..

"A part of all you earn is YOURS to keep" - George Clason, "The   Richest   Man   in   Babylon"

You have to pay yourself first. This is a very important principle and it is how you will start building wealth. It will also be your emergency fund. Every time you get paid, deposit someportion of that money in your savings account, before you pay anyone else (whether it is taxes, expenses, debts etc).

You need to consider two things:

1- Treat it just like any other bill. Deposit money every month, even if it's only $25. Deposit more when you can. Once you make it a habit, this account will grow very quickly;

2- NEVER withdraw money from this account (unless, of course, you have a real life emergency that you cannot cover with your income). If you do make a withdrawal, make sure you "pay yourself back" as soon as possible. Hold a garage sale, sell stuff you no longer need, do whatever it takes to replenish the money you took out, AS SOON AS POSSIBLE. Otherwise, let it grow <u>at least</u> for a few years. Once you are debt-free, you can use this money as a down payment for a house, or any other investment. This is <u>critical</u>! Note: a birthday present is NOT an emergency. The idea is to have money in case you need to repair your car, for example, so you don't deviate from your debt elimination plan.

Step 7- Fill out the debt elimination chart, and put the Debt Elimination Program into practice right away.

You will find a copy of the debt elimination chart at the end of this book. You will need it for this exercise. During your Debt Elimination Program you will be focusing <u>on one account at a time</u> and you will be making minimum payments on all others. *This is crucial for your success.*

When you send an extra $40 to a credit card company, an extra $25 with your car payment and an extra $20 to another account, you are only diluting your efforts. If you tackle many accounts at once, you may feel like you are not accomplishing much because you don't see tangible results. And you will feel discouraged. With this program, you will be focusing on one account at a time until it's paid off. In this example, you will send an extra $85 to one account instead of $40, $25 and $20 to three different accounts.

Now proceed to fill out the debt elimination chart as explained below to determine the order in which the accounts will be paid off.

Look at the chart below as you follow along. The concept is very simple: You will determine the order in which your accounts will be paid off based on a simple formula, and you will pay off one account at a time.

By now you should have determined how much extra money you can dedicate every month to your Debt Elimination Program (we'll call it your "Power Payment"). If possible, I strongly recommend you dedicate 10% of your income to your "Power Payment". For some people this will be easy, for others it may be a little harder. Try to do it at least until you have paid off a few accounts.

As an example, we will use Jonathan and Tracy's chart, from San Diego. They are using $400 as their Power Payment. Their combined yearly income is $70,000. This is the chart that they filled out, based on their financial situation.

NOTE: if your budget only allows $100 or $200 a month it will still work, it will just take longer. The higher your Power Payment, the faster you will get out of debt.

1		2	3	4	5	6	7
	Debt	Total Owed	Minimum monthly payment	Column 2 ÷ Column 3	Priority	Power Payment	Months to pay off 2 ÷ 6
1	Mastercard	$3,150.00	$126.00	25	5	959+126= $1085	3

2	Mastercard	$8,200.00	$328.00	25	6	1085+328= $1413	6
3	Visa	$2,200.00	$76.00	25	4	883+76= $959	2
4	Discover	$800.00	$32.00	25	3	851+32= $883	1
5	Dept Store	$630.00	$26.00	25	2	825+26= $851	1
6	Car 1	$10,200.00	$425.00	24	1	400+425= $825	12
7	Car 2	$15,000.00	$480.00	31	7	1413+480= $1893	8
8	Heloc	$30,000.00	$350.00	86	8	1893+350= $2243	14
9	Mortgage	$150,000.00	$1,079.00	128	9	2243+1079 = $3322	45
	Total	$220,180				Total	92

HOW TO FILL IT OUT:

- On the first column of your chart, write down the accounts in which you have outstanding balances.

- On column #2, write down the current balance. On column #3, enter the minimum monthlypayment.

- On column #4, divide column #2 by column #3, and enter the resulting number there. This will be the approximate number of months that it will take you to pay off the loan by paying only the minimum payment. The amount is NOT exact but it's here only to determine the order in which you will be paying off your accounts. Now look at this column and look for the lowest number; this will be the account you will pay off first. For credit cards, please note that banks usually require a minimum payment equal to 2% to 4% of your balance (there are exceptions); that's why in this example the number is 25 for all credit cards on column #4. If this is your case and you also have more than one account with the same number, just focus on the account with the lowest balance FIRST.

- On column # 5, enter the priority based on column #4, lowest numbers first.

- Now, column #6 is where you will enter, for your first account (in this example, the one highlighted on column #5), your "Power Payment" + the minimum payment for that account. In this case it would be $435 (minimum payment) + $400 (Power Payment) = $835 total payment. Now this account will be paid off in just over 12 months.

Then proceed to send the minimum payment to all accounts, and the minimum + your Power Payment to your account #1 (on column 5) until this account is paid off. Once it is paid off, then you are going to target account #2 (also on column 5), adding your Power Payment + the minimum payment you were sending before to your first account. In this example, for account #2, it would be $835 ($400 Power Payment + $435 minimum payment you were sending before to account #1, now paid off) + $27 (minimum payment for account #2). Keep working this plan until all accounts are paid off. You will get out of debt, all accounts paid off (including your mortgage) in record time! How will you feel once you are debt-free?

A few things you can do that will help you with your plan:

Put your debt elimination chart in a place where you can see it often

As soon as an account is paid off, use a red marker and cross it off, or write PAID OFF (and the DATE) in big, red letters

Also, every time you pay off an account, go celebrate! Take your spouse (or significant other) out to dinner and feel the power of your determination and persistence.

As you see the progress you are making on your chart, think (with emotion) "I am becoming debt-free". Feel how it feels to be debt free. Pat yourself on the shoulder for a job well done! (Do it, it works!)

Remember these extreme situations require extreme solutions and sacrifices, so if you need to, work extra hours, get a second job, hold garage sales, sell stuff you can live without, unsubscribe from services you don't really need, etc. If your car is paid off, resist the temptation to buy another one (for as long as possible). You get the idea.

Make sure your savings account has at least $2000 as an emergency fund. Add any extra money you can to your Power Payment and to your savings, but do not withdraw from your savings except for an emergency. If you do, replenish it ASAP.

Every day, several times a day, say to yourself: "I am wealth, I am abundance, I am health, I am joy". Feel it deep inside, feel the abundance surrounding you. This was taken from an excellent book called "A happy pocket full of money". Or pick a phrase you believe in, and repeat it to yourself, with feelings, several times a day like a mantra.

Remember, keeping up with the Jones' (other people who are in debt) will only make you a slave to debt for life. Now you know you can control your debt. Once you start your debt elimination plan, you will feel the power that comes from being in control of your finances. You can live your life by design and create a bright future for yourself and your family.

Now that you understand the step-by-step plan to get out of debt, commit yourself to doing it. You deserve to be debt-free!

LESSON #4

UNDERSTAND YOUR OPTIONS: FROM CREDIT COUNSELING TO VARIOUS DEBT SETTLEMENT OPTIONS

There seems to be a widespread misconception about what a credit counselor can and cannot do for you, so let's start by explaining what Credit Counseling is and then we'll explain what Debt Settlement is.

Credit Counselors will not settle your debts, that is not what they do. What they can do for you is consolidate your unsecured debts and lower your interest rates, and then collect a payment from you through a debt management plan.

Credit Counseling, when done through a reputable company, can be a great help to get out of debt. It is also known as Debt Consolidation since the idea is to consolidate all your unsecured debts into one account, and you send only one payment every month to the Credit Counseling company who in return forwards it to your creditors. They usually charge a fee of about $35-$60 per month for their services and you can expect to be debt free within 5 years. They will negotiate a lower rate for you (about 7-9 % or so, depending on several factors) which can sometimes be a huge reduction (keep in mind that some people are paying 23% or more!). When you start the process, you will be asked to cut up your credit cards which is always a good thing to do when you are in debt (regardless of whether you do debt consolidation or not!).

You will probably not be able to get new credit until your accounts are paid off (let's face it, who would give you credit if they see in your credit report that you haven't been able to pay the other creditors?) but the great thing is that you know you can be debt free in a few short years.

A good credit counseling company will do what its name implies, they will teach you how to handle your finances, and many will even offer financial classes to help you understand how to manage your money properly.

The challenge is that many credit counseling agencies may not have your best interest in mind. I know this for a fact, since I once started working for a Credit Counseling company in San Diego and had to resign on my second day when I became aware of their unethical practices. I simply would never be part of a company that takes advantage of the people it is supposed to be helping. I told the owner what I thought and resigned; it was clear to me that he was in that business just for the money (and he was making A LOT of it!). To find a legitimate credit counselor, go to the National Foundation for Credit Counseling at http://www.nfcc.org

Debt settlement, on the other hand, is when a creditor forgives a portion of your debt if they think that they will not be able to collect the total amount. The reasoning is simple: it's better to collect something than nothing.

Obviously not everybody will be able to settle their debts. A person may be successful settling one debt but maybe another credit card may not be willing to settle. If you can convince them with enough facts that you absolutely cannot pay the entire amount, then you have a very good chance of reaching a good settlement.

Since a credit card settlement will show up as a negative on your credit report, this option is not for you if you are paying your bills on time, have a good record and would like to keep it that way.

Please note that debt settlement should ONLY be used as a last resource if you are considering bankruptcy; the process can sometimes be difficult and its effectiveness will depend on many factors. It's like doing your own taxes. Yes, you can do it, but you will never know how much better would have been if it was done by a professional. Almost always it would be done much better by a professional.

I strongly suggest that if you decide to go on this route and decide to try to settle your debts, you must hire a professional to do the job for you. This way you will be way ahead of the game, since a professional has been through the process many times and has the experience necessary to reach a good settlement agreement on your behalf.

Keep in mind that collectors are people who have been trained to collect money, they do it every day for a living, so they do know what they are doing. They are used to negotiating with people, and they have been through different scenarios and situations. So the best option is to hire somebody who is used to dealing with these trained collectors and knows how to play their game.

Just be very careful since there are a lot of crooks out there it's always better to go with a company or attorney that was referred to you by somebody who can give you good references about their services.

But if you do decide to do it yourself, here are some guidelines that will help you achieve very good results.

Settling will only work if your account is seriously past due. Companies will only offer a good settlement option when they believe it's their last chance to recover their money. When they think that if they don't settle, they won't recover a penny of the money you owe. Usually, the best time to start negotiating a debt settlement is about 4 or 5 months after you sent your last payment. Remember that at about 6 months or less they will probably sell your account to a collection agency, so do not wait for more than 5 months. Once the account is sold to the collection agency, you will lose most of your leverage. You can still settle, but it's not the same, the sense of "urgency" that the credit card company had before is now lost.

Most settlements are between 30% and 70% of the amount owed. It will depend on several factors, mostly on your negotiation skills and how long it has been since you sent your last payment. You may want to offer 20%, but expect your offer to be rejected. Your goal should be to settle for about 50% of your debt, but settling for 2/3rds can be a reasonable goal. Keep in mind that people who actually settle for 10-20% are the exception to the rule; very few people accomplish this.

Before you talk to them, make sure you have all the paperwork you need in front of you:

-all copies of your statements, letters from your creditors, and a dedicated notepad where you can take notes of everything you discuss during your conversation. Remember to always write down the date and time of the call, the name of the person you talked to, their number or extension if they can provide it, and everything you talked about.

This is one of the most critical factors here: <u>always</u>, no matter what they say and how much they threaten you, <u>ALWAYS be nice to them</u>. Never, EVER use profane language or threats; it will only make you lose your battle. The key is to always be nice and treat them with respect. If you deviate from this even for a moment, you lose.

Make sure you get all offers in writing. Whatever you talk on the phone, if you don't get it in writing, is useless. Anytime they offer a deal you find acceptable, make sure you ask them to send it to you in writing.

Occasionally you may talk to somebody who might not be willing to negotiate, or who will treat you in a disrespectful way. In this case, you can either politely terminate the call, or ask to speak to a supervisor. But again, always be very polite and respectful, and never use profane language or threats.

Ask them to remove all late fees, finance charges and over the limit fees from your account. This alone will reduce your balance substantially. Do not demand, always ask politely. "You know, I would really like to pay you all that I owe, but I simply can't. I lost my job and have very limited income (or whatever your situation is). But if we can get the balance to be more manageable for me, I am willing to start sending you payments starting this week". If they see that you are sincere and willing to pay them, you have more chances that they will be willing to help you.

You will be talking (mostly) to trained professionals. They go through extensive training on how to collect money and how to ask the right questions to get the information they want. So never lie to them. Just be sincere, you want to pay but you don't have the means, but if they can help you by reducing the total balance you will be happy to pay them. This is the attitude that will help you.

Always start with a goal in mind. What would be a good amount to settle for? Say you owe $10,000 to a credit card company. A good number would be $5,000 (50%) or less, but it will depend on many factors. So if they offer you to settle for $8,000 you can politely decline, because it would "probably" be better just to file bankruptcy (again, if they feel they will lose it all because you are filing for bankruptcy, they may concede). Many times you will get a phone call or a letter a few days later offering to settle for less.

Keep in mind that they will almost always run your credit report and look at your payment history. So if you are paying all your bills on time but not to XYZ Company, then XYZ will not be willing to settle with you. After all, if you are paying everybody else, chances are you can pay them as well. But if they see in your report that you have not been paying most of your bills for over three months, or four months, then they will most likely be willing to settle with you. If they see it's their last chance to recover their money, then you have the leverage. But this is a two-edge sword as it can backfire on you if you don't know how to negotiate properly.

There are four factors critical to the success of the debt-settlement negotiation process: Communicating effectively, Negotiating, Documenting and Following Up. When you excel in all four you will walk away with great results.

When you agree to send a payment, many times the collector will ask you to pay right then, while you are on the phone. It is very important that you do not do so: <u>make sure they send you the offer in writing FIRST; then you mail them the check</u>. You can say something like this: "I understand you want a payment right now, but unfortunately I cannot make a payment at this time, it is just not possible. I will have $_____ soon and want to settle at least one of my accounts with whoever will give me the best deal. Could you please send me an offer in writing?" The amount you mention in your conversation should be a round number representing about 30-50% of your balance, or whatever you can pay at the time.

This is worth repeating many times, because it's critical to your success. Always be kind, nice and polite. Be sincere and never lie. Even though many collectors will not care, make sure they understand your situation. "I would love to pay you but I have been (laid off, in the hospital, with a reduced salary, got divorced, etc). I am desperate and I'm seriously considering filing for bankruptcy".

Every time you send them anything (whether a letter or a payment) use Certified Mail with return receipt. Remember that <u>documentation</u> is extremely important; it is one of the four factors that will determine how successful you are.

So this is the debt settlement process. It is not hard, but most people will probably have better results if they go with a trained professional. If you do decide to do it yourself, make sure you read this chapter several times, leave nothing to chance and do your research first! Study the steps & write down what you are going to tell them.

LESSON #5

THE HIDDEN PSYCHOLOGY OF MONEY & WEALTH — CHANGING YOUR MINDSET TO ACQUIRE WEALTH

"Whatever you believe with emotion becomes your reality. You always act in a manner consistent with your innermost beliefs and convictions"

- Brian Tracy

I am sure that this piece of the book is more essential than the well ordered arrangement we have recently portrayed. To me, it doesn't make sense to show you how to get out of debt unless you can change your mindset about what is possible for you. Once you change your mindset and you get out of debt, <u>nothing can stop you</u>.

I found that most of the time when we fail to achieve what we really want, there is an underlying belief (that we are usually not aware of) that is not supporting us. Have you ever experienced self-sabotage? Have you ever failed to follow through on something that you wanted to achieve? Most likely you had conflicting beliefs that were pulling you in different directions.

BUT WHAT IS A BELIEF?

A belief is a feeling of certainty about what something means to you. Most of our beliefs are generalizations about our past that are based on interpretations of our experiences. In other words, they are based on how we interpreted what happened to us at the moment. Let me give you an example. Twin brothers go to an amusement park and decide to take a ride on a roller-coaster together. One walks out of that ride feeling very happy and thrilled, and these effects will be positive over his lifetime. The other, however, walks out of that same ride full of fear and shock, and those effects will be negative for him over his lifetime. It was the same ride, but it was perceived differently by them. We all perceive and interpret our experiences in a different way.

Which brings me to another very important point that you should always remember: it is not **what happens** to us in life, but **how we interpret** what happens to us and what we decide to **focus on** that changes our life. We need to take responsibility for where we are in life, feel grateful for it and move on. Blaming our situation or our "conditions" will only bring more of the same. By feeling grateful for what you have, whatever that may be, you are actually impressing thoughts of abundance upon the Universe, and the Universe will deliver to you more abundance. It may sound strange to some people, but it is one of the immutable Laws of the Universe, the Law of Attraction. For more information on the Law of Attraction, see the Resources section.

But let's go back to your beliefs and how they affect your life. They actually affect everything you do, since all your actions

58

are the result of your beliefs. They are extremely important to achieving success in anything you do.

You see, from the day we are born we are being thrown at with negative suggestions. Not knowing how to counter them, we unconsciously accept them and bring them into being as our experience.

For example, we are told:

- You cannot do it / You can't do that

- You don't have a chance

- Things are only getting worse

- You may get fired

- You are not smart enough

And so on. Get the idea?

Consider now the fact that right now in America, there are about 36 million people that are 65 years of age and older. Out of that 36 million people, over 34 million are broke. They are depending on someone else for life's necessities.

Why is it that in the richest country in the world, 95% of the population ends up broke?

If you ask these people, they would tell you that their lives were shaped by exterior forces or circumstances, by things that happened to them. This implies that they were not in control, that they were merely a leaf in the wind.

But as we said before, and it's so important that it is worth repeating, it is not **whathappens** to us in life, but **how weinterpret** what happens to us and what we decide to **focus on** that changes our life. A person's fortune can be completely wiped out, and he or she can build it again with the right mindset. It has happened millions of times, which proves that it is NOT <u>what</u> happens to you but <u>how</u> you react to it.

The main reason that most people never achieve financial independence is that we are not taught how to succeed. We are not taught how to achieve financial independence. We are not taught how to handle money. We are never taught that WE are in charge of our lives.

The educational system in place today was created in the 1800's, and was designed to prepare us to work as employees. In high school, we are not taught how to handle money, how to invest it, how to create passive streams of income. We don't learn it either in College or University. We grow up (most of us, anyway) believing that money is in short supply, is hard to come by and that you have to work really hard for it. We grow up associating different things to money like "If I have a lot of money, I may lose my friends," thereby, "money equals loneliness." Other common beliefs are "money changes people, they become greedy", "If I make a lot of money, I could lose my motivation". Or, "If I'm broke (or poor) people will pay more attention to me". And the list goes on and on.

The fact is that money by itself is neither good or bad. It is what we associate to money that makes all the difference in the world.

Let me give you a few examples that affected me personally.

I lived most of my life under a set of beliefs that controlled most of what I did. It took me a while to identify those beliefs, but when I did, I realized that they had such an enormous power over me that they controlled my focus, my ideas, and my acts. Before I was aware of these beliefs, I blamed my circumstances on other people or "bad luck".

When I was growing up, money was always tight. My father lost his job when I was 8 years old. He could never get another job that paid him enough, so we were always short of money. My parents had no choice but to take me out of private school and send me to public school. I remember my parents saying to me, "we are middle class", and as a kid, I accepted it as if it were a fact that would never change.

Growing up in an environment of lack, I felt that money was in short supply. That money only went to other people richer than me. People said that "money can't buy you happiness", and I believed it. I deeply believed that because of circumstances that were beyond my control, other people could have money, but not me. I believed I was "middle class", period. I was "destined" to be that way.

Let me ask you, how do you think living with these beliefs affected my life as an adult? How did it affect what was possible or impossible for me?

At a conscious level, I wanted to earn a lot of money so I could live comfortably. But deep inside me, (at a subconscious level) I never believed I could earn good money. When I worked as a salesperson many years ago, I would have a great week, and then during the next 3 weeks I would sabotage my own success. I would not work hard until the money ran out. This was done subconsciously of course; there was always a "reasonable" excuse for not working hard.

I am very grateful to the Universe for the parents I have and the experiences I had, since they prepared me for what I am today.

The truth of the matter is that all beliefs that we "inherit" from our parents, are beliefs that they "inherited" from *their* parents.

So I now choose to believe things that will inspire me, and I do not really care if they are factual truths or not; they will become truths once I believe in them.

A couple of examples of my new beliefs are:

- I am a soul with a body; my soul is infinitely abundant

- I am always surrounded by abundance. Abundance is all there is.

- Money always comes easily and effortlessly

- I am wealth – I am abundance – I am health

You have beliefs about everything. What's more, what is incredible about distinguishing and changing your beliefs, is that you can think anything that can help you accomplish your objectives.

You have to look for those limiting beliefs that are controlling your life. If you are ready to break free from the chains of limiting beliefs, I will guide you through a simple yet very powerful process that will enable you to change those beliefs for good.

You can literally change anything you want.

To get the best results out of the following exercise, you will need a quiet place and privacy.

If you are in debt, you need to adopt new beliefs that will empower you. You can decide what you will choose to believe, so why not find beliefs that will help you achieve your goals? Beliefs that limit your actions can be as devastating as positive beliefs can be empowering. When we fully believe something is true, it is like delivering a command to our brain as to how to represent what is occurring. In other words, they are "filters" to our perceptions of the world.

We need to take responsibility for where we are in life. We need to stop blaming others for what happens to us, and decide to move forward.

A few good beliefs to have are:

- Everything happens for a good reason (even if, right now, I cannot see what that good reason is)

- People are inherently good

- Money is easy to come by

- The Universe is abundant and limitless, and money never runs out

- Even before a problem occurs, it has already been solved. There is a solution to it somewhere, and I will find it.

- I am wealth – I am abundance – I am health

- I am a spirit with a body; my spirit is eternally abundant and wealthy

- Being broke is only temporary.

Feel free to come up with any beliefs that will empower you, in all areas of your life.

There are several ways to change beliefs on purpose. The following method is the one I found to be the most effective. It involves associating a lot of emotional pain to the old belief, and a lot of emotional pleasure to the new belief. This is a process you do only once for the belief to be replaced with an empowering one of your choice.

Now let's start the process of changing our old beliefs. Let me warn you though, that just reading this exercise will not change anything in your life! You DO NEED to complete this exercise. Believe me, it will be fun, and it will not take long. And you can do it as many times as you want, any time you discover a belief that is not empowering you.

A way to identify a belief is this: they are usually found after the word "because", on phrases you usually say. As an example, if you hear yourself saying something like, "I will always be fat, *because* my father and mother are overweight, and I have their genes". Another example, "They wouldn't give me that job, *because* I am not smart enough". Or, "I could never succeed, *because* I never succeeded before in my life". Do you get the idea?

Let's start with your limiting beliefs. Write down 5 beliefs that you have about yourself and what you are capable of. What are five beliefs that have limited you in the past? i.e., "I could never make more than $50,000 a year", " I can't get a better job", "nobody would pay me that much", etc.

1_____

2_____

3_____

4_____

5_____

Now you write down 5 empowering beliefs that can now support you in achieving your goals. Do not limit yourself in your new beliefs. Think big, think bold! Also, and this is extremely important, <u>state your beliefs in the affirmative</u>, never state a belief that negates what you don't want. Example: "My life is abundant" is a great example, but "I don't have any more debt" is not, since it is not positive enough, and your brain will focus on "debt" instead of the "I don't". These new beliefs will replace the ones that have limited you before.

1_____

2_____

3_____

4

5_____

Excellent! Feel grateful for taking this first step that can change your life for the better.

Now, get two pieces of paper. On the first piece of paper, write down the first limiting belief you are eliminating. What you are going to do first is create doubt. Once you start to doubt a belief, it becomes weak, making it easier to replace with another belief. Then, you are going to associate massive pain to having that belief, and massive pain in the future if you continue to have that belief. In other words, you have to feel the negative emotions associated with living with that belief, and how it would negatively affect you. Then, on the other piece of paper, you are going to associate massive pleasure to the new belief that you want to adopt in its place.

This exercise is extremely powerful, so please, do yourself a favor and take it seriously. You can change your life now.

Let's start with the first belief. You have already written this belief down on the first piece of paper; now ask yourself the following questions:

1- How is this belief ridiculous or absurd?

2- What negative consequences have you already experienced as a result of having this RIDICULOUS belief? What has it cost you emotionally, financially, physically and in your relationships in the past, because of having this ABSURD belief?

3- What is it costing you now, emotionally, financially, physically and in your relationships, because of having this WRONG belief?

4- What will it cost you emotionally, financially, physically, in your relationships, during the next 10 years, if you don't let go of this belief now?

Write down everything that comes to your mind. Keep writing about all the pain you experienced in your past, all the pain you are experiencing right now, and all the pain you will be experiencing in the future if you don't change this **absurd** belief now.

Make sure you feel as much pain as possible. Feel all the negative emotions associated with having this absurd belief. Close your eyes and visualize it, live it, feel it as if it were happening right now. I know this doesn't sound very appealing, but believe me, you will be amazed at the results!

Once you are fully associated with the pain that having this belief has cost you and would have cost you your whole life, get the second piece of paper, and write down the new empowering belief that will take the place of the old one.

Ask yourself the following questions:

- How will having this empowering belief affect my life?

- What benefits will I get from having this empowering belief?

- How will I feel and how will I act by having this empowering belief?

- Where will I be in 10 years as a result of having this empowering belief?

Imagine yourself 10 years from now, and looking back at the last 10 years, how does it feel having lived with this empowering belief? Stay there for a while, feeling those great feelings.

While you are writing down each answer, make sure you fully associate with the positive feelings of having this empowering belief. Feel how much better your life is as a result of having this belief. Close your eyes and feel it in your body. How would you feel? How would you move? How would you breathe?

The key here is to experience as much pleasure as possible.

Now grab the first piece of paper containing your old beliefs, and burn it. As you see the paper burning, feel the old belief vanishing in your past, and feel the power of your new belief.

Congratulations! Feel grateful for having a great, empowering belief that will support you for the rest of your life.

Do the same with the next belief, and keep repeating until you finish replacing all your old beliefs.

This exercise was adapted from similar exercises by Anthony Robbins and Bob Proctor.

ANOTHER WAY TO REPLACE LIMITING BELIEFS

I recently found another way to change beliefs and counter negative suggestions that I use very frequently. It is incredibly powerful and it also helps me to keep on being focused on what I want.

Even though I used affirmations in the past, they never seemed to work for me. Throughout the years I heard about how important it was to repeat to yourself the "right" affirmations, and since I never noticed any benefits I quit doing it.

But it wasn't until I watched the movie "You can heal your life" by Louis Hayes that I finally "got it". In the movie, a person who got cured of cancer explained that she was repeating an affirmation 400 times a day. Four hundred times a day! That's why it worked for her; her subconscious mind ended up believing what she was affirming. It never worked for me because I would repeat my affirmations only a few times a day (no wonder, right?)

So one day I found a cheap Mardi Gras bead necklace that was given to me at a party and I thought to myself: "This would be great to use while I practice my affirmations". It has 88 beads, so I would repeat one affirmation out loud about 100 times while I was going through the necklace on my way to work every morning, with emotion and feeling it as if it was already real. Then, on my way back home, I would repeat the process. It was a total of about 200 affirmations a day, but I wanted to find a way to double that.

So what I did was to shorten the affirmations without modifying their meaning, and also to write them down whenever I could. Their benefits were incredible! It took about three weeks to start seeing the benefits, but then I got hooked. I would do one affirmation for at least three weeks before moving on to the next one.

The best way I found is to start the affirmations with "I'm so happy and grateful now that…" and fill in the blanks with whatever you want to achieve or get. Some examples could be:

"I'm so happy and grateful now that I'm driving my …. (name/model of car you want)"

"I'm so happy and grateful now that I get up at 5:00 AM fully energized"

"I'm so happy and grateful now that I weigh 175 lbs (or whatever you want)

"I'm so happy and grateful now that my Chase MasterCard is fully paid off"

"I'm so happy and grateful now that money comes easily and frequently"

Write down a list of affirmations and pick one to start with. Repeat your affirmation out loud, 200 to 400 times a day. It's Ok to try different tones of voice since you will probably get tired after a while. I found that it works ten times better to say them out loud than in your head, so say them out loud as many times as possible.

How to use affirmations effectively

In his book, "The spiritual basis of real prosperity", Roy Eugene Davis says about affirmations:

"Mechanical repetition of affirmations is a waste of time. Speak with deliberate, soul-felt conviction until super conscious awareness of the reality of that which is affirmed is clear and unwavering". In other words, live the affirmation as if it were true, with deep emotion and conviction (excellent book to read by the way).

At the beginning it will probably feel weird and your brain may go: "liar, you know this is not true!" but keep going. After a while, your subconscious mind will start accepting it. And once your subconscious mind believes it, your life will start to change.

CHANGING YOUR "MONEY MINDSET"

Remember what the definition of insanity is? Doing the same thing over and over and expecting a different result.

If you want things to change, YOU have to change first. You can be in control of your life by choosing what to focus on most of the time.

Successful people choose to focus on positive things; unsuccessful people focus on negative things by default.

SO… DO WHAT SUCCESSFUL PEOPLE DO!

Spend most of your time focusing on positive things, NOT on negative things.

<u>Focus on what you want to achieve</u>, NOT on what you do not want to achieve.

<u>Focus on what you like</u>, NOT on what you don't like.

Before I learned this lesson I would curse every fault of the car I owned at the time. The more I focused on it, the more miserable I felt. When I learned to be thankful for the car, I changed my mindset and I felt better.

I am not saying to ignore your problems. Acknowledge your problems, but don't dwell on them.

Be thankful for the problem since, most likely, it is an opportunity in disguise. You can find the greatest opportunities of your life "hidden" in your worst moments. That's why all successful people see problems as opportunities.

The best advice I can give you is to reframe every "difficulty". That means that you find the good in a seemingly "bad" situation.

Always focus on abundance, not lack or problems. Focus on wealth building, not surviving. Focus on your next check, not your last one.

When you find yourself thinking about the negative aspects of your life, immediately replace the negative thoughts with a positive one, like a mantra. If you catch yourself saying, "I can't afford it," immediately say "I couldn't afford it in the past, but I can afford it now. I just choose not to buy it at this time," or something similar. You don't have to believe it yet. You can "fake it 'til you make it."

Feel abundance in your life and be grateful for your abundance. What you focus on expands. If you focus on lack, it expands. When you focus on abundance, it expands as well.

Remember, abundance isn't just about money. You may have an abundance of friends, health, faith or ideas. Look at nature. Everywhere you turn there is abundance. Life, by its very nature, is abundant. Just open your eyes; open your mind.

OF COURSE THIS IS EASIER SAID THAN DONE, SO HOW TO START?

There are several things you can do right away:

Start meditating every day. Even if you don't know how to meditate, at least find a quiet spot, sit comfortably, close your eyes, and breathe deeply. Focus on your breathing. Stay like this for a few minutes, and avoid any thoughts; just focus on your breathing. Then visualize a goal you want to achieve, and feel as if you have already achieved it. FEEL what it feels like to have achieved that goal. Make it as real as possible. Touch it, feel it, smell it, see it. Stay in that feeling for a few minutes, and thank the Universe for having achieved it. This is probably the most powerful exercise you can do to become successful.

Read positive books, every single day. At least read for 15 minutes, preferably for 30 minutes or more. I always read before going to bed, so I can go to sleep with positive thoughts and feelings.

Listen to positive CDs in your car instead of music (or what's worse, the news!)

Avoid the news, negative people, negative movies, negative talk shows and anything that will affect you negatively. Feed your mind with positive things every day.

Feel genuinely grateful for what you have. FEEL deep feelings of gratitude. This is incredibly powerful, so do not take it lightly. Feel grateful for anything you have, your car (even if you don't like it, still feel grateful for having it), your kids, your spouse, a flower, etc. Feel grateful every day. Write down a list of things you are grateful for, and as you are writing, feel the gratitude. Do it for 5-10 minutes every day. Make sure that as soon as you wake up, you think about things to be grateful for. It's the best way to start your day!

Surround yourself with positive people that inspire you. This is very important! One way could be to start a mastermind group, where all of you can share ideas and support each other. You can either meet at somebody's house once a week or at a restaurant. You can even do a conference call once a week if some of you live in different cities. You can also find a mentor that can help you stay focused or new friends that share the same goals.

Feel the abundance that surrounds you. Even if at this moment you don't have the money you want, you can find abundance if you look for it. Abundance is not just money; abundance is everywhere. Maybe you have an abundance of love? Or an abundance of friends? Look for abundance in Nature. Look at the ocean, you will see abundance. Look at trees, you will see abundance. Just FEEL abundance instead of lack, and you will attract it.

Take workshops when possible, take classes if you can. Find an Adult School. Their classes are free.

Rememeber this: You can make your life a masterpiece. Just focus on it, every day. And always, ALWAYS, be grateful for what you have.

There is NOTHING that you cannot be, do, or have. You are a magnificent human being with unlimited potential. Do not settle for mediocrity, you deserve more!

RESOURCES

#1: GET OUT OF DEBT CHART

My Power Payment will be _____   Start Date _____

My plan to become debt-free

Debt	Total Owed	Minimum monthly payment	Column 2 ÷ Column 3	Priority	Power Payment	Months to pay off 2 ÷ 6
	2	3	4	5	6	7
otal					Total	

I will be debt-free in _____ months

#2: BUDGET SPREADSHEET

Income	
Salary / Commissions	
Overtime / Bonuses	
Other	
Monthly Total	

Expenses		Balance	Interest Rate
Rent / Mortgage			
Food / Supermarket			
Utilities			
Electric / Gas			
Water			
Cable			
Internet			
Phone			
Cell Phones			
Misc.			
Car related			
Car payment			
Car payment			
Car insurance			
Gas			
Car expenses			
Misc			
Credit Cards			
CC1			
CC2			
CC3			
CC4			
CC5			
Alimony			
School Tuition			
Clothing			
Food (eating out)			
Student Loans			
Misc (describe)			
-			
-			
-			
-			
Total Expenses		Total Income	
		Total Expenses	

Total [   ]

CONCLUSION

I want to thank you again for buying this book. I really hope it inspires you in taking action, do what is needed and finally crawl out of the debt spiral you are facing.

Remember that you have the power to alter your life and overcome any obstacle. Use the steps in this book to do it. Gradually, you will find that the odds are stacked up in your favor. Dilligence, hard work and discipline are all key to getting out of debt. You can do it, I know you can. The mere fact that you bought this book shows you're on the right path. So feel good about yourself.

By taking some very simple measures, acting responsively and being accountable – you can get out of debt soon enough, and enjoy the freedom that being debt-free entails.

I wish you all the best!

Adam Watkins..